Walter Foster
Jr.

learn to draw
Zoo Animals

Step-by-step instructions for more than 25 zoo animals

ILLUSTRATED BY ROBBIN CUDDY

Quarto is the authority on a wide range of topics.
Quarto educates, entertains, and enriches the lives of our readers—
enthusiasts and lovers of hands-on living.
www.quartoknows.com

© 2016 Quarto Publishing Group USA Inc.
Published by Walter Foster Jr., an imprint of Quarto Publishing Group USA Inc.
All rights reserved. Walter Foster Jr. is trademarked.
Photographs © Shutterstock
Written by Elizabeth T. Gilbert
Page Layout by Steve Scott

6 Orchard Road, Suite 100
Lake Forest, CA 92630
quartoknows.com
Visit our blogs @quartoknows.com

Printed in China
3 5 7 9 10 8 6 4 2

Table of Contents

Tools & Materials

There's more than one way to bring zoo animals to life on paper—you can use crayons, markers, colored pencils, or even paints. Just be sure you have plenty of animal colors—grays, browns, blacks, oranges, and reds.

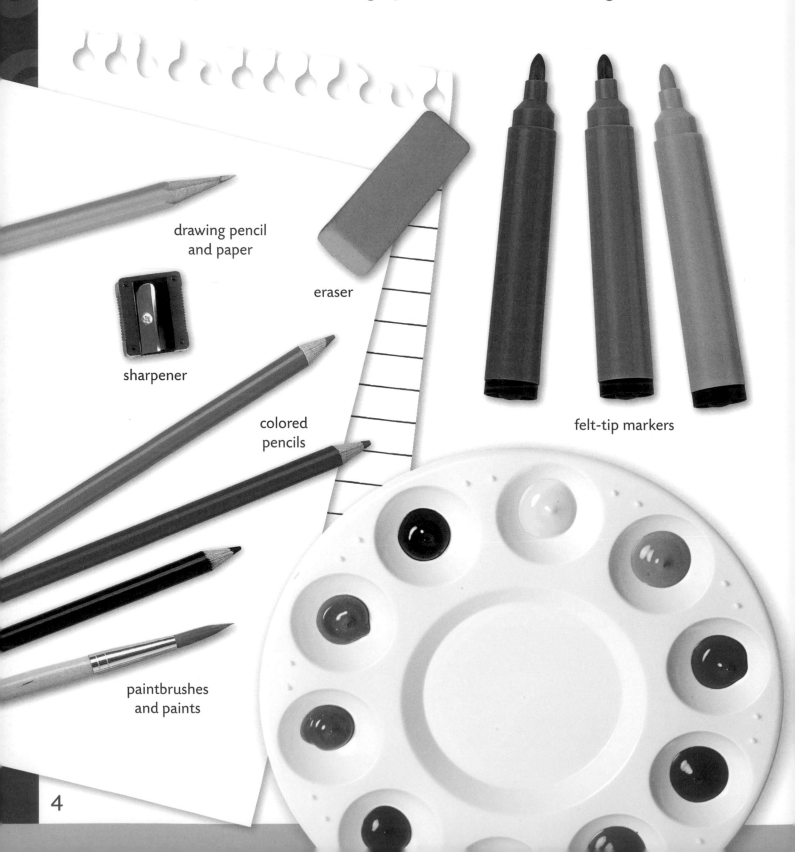

drawing pencil
and paper

eraser

sharpener

colored
pencils

felt-tip markers

paintbrushes
and paints

How to Use This Book

The drawings in this book are made up of basic shapes, such as circles, triangles, and rectangles. Practice drawing the shapes below.

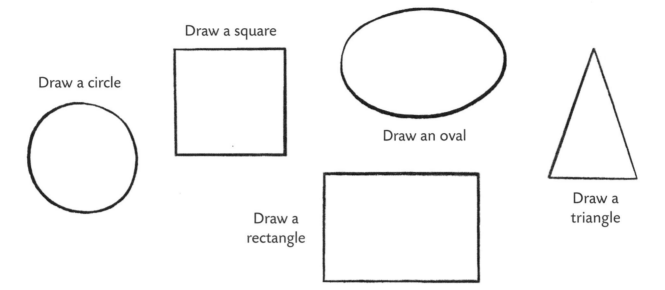

Draw a circle

Draw a square

Draw an oval

Draw a rectangle

Draw a triangle

Notice how these drawings begin with basic shapes.

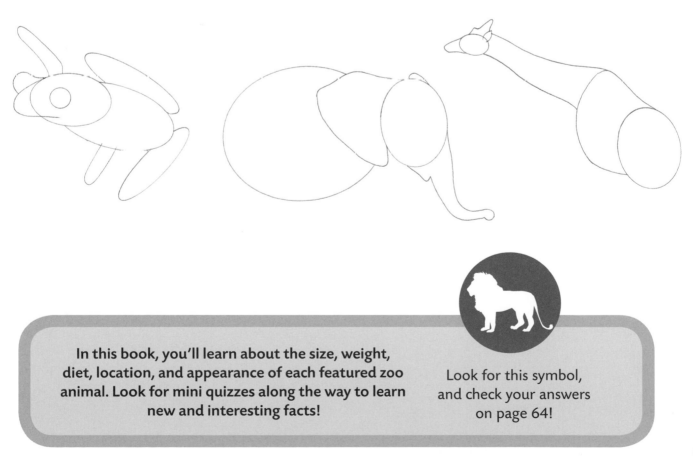

In this book, you'll learn about the size, weight, diet, location, and appearance of each featured zoo animal. Look for mini quizzes along the way to learn new and interesting facts!

Look for this symbol, and check your answers on page 64!

Zoo Animals of the World

Zoos are safe places where you can experience exciting animals from all over the world, from an Australian wallaby to an African lion. Before you learn to draw them, view the map below to see where the animals in this book can be found in the wild.

North America

Europe

South America

Asia

Africa

Australia

Lion

Size: 6.5 feet long
Weight: 500 pounds
Diet: Hoofed animals, baboons, rodents, and water buffalo
Location: Sub-Saharan Africa and India

Fun Fact!

Lions are fast runners and skilled hunters, but they sure enjoy their cat naps! It is estimated that lions sleep up to 20 hours a day.

The lion is a large, muscular feline with a tuft of hair at the end of its tail. A male lion has a fluffy mane around its neck and a deep, distinct roar.

Mini Quiz
What is the name for a group of lions that live and hunt together?
A. Pride
B. Colony
C. Pod
D. Band
(Answer on page 64)

Elephant

Diet: Grass, leaves, and fruit

Size: Up to 13 feet tall at the shoulder

Weight: 12,000 to 18,000 pounds

Did You Know?

The trunk is a very sensitive organ made up of 16 muscles and lots of nerves. This hand-like organ helps an elephant eat, drink, breathe, smell, spray water, greet other elephants, and more!

Location: Africa and Asia

The elephant is an intelligent pachyderm with a long trunk, a pair of ivory tusks, thick skin, large ears, and a skinny tail.

Fun Fact!
You can easily tell the difference between an African elephant and an Asian elephant by their ears! African elephants' are much larger, which helps them stay cool in hot temperatures.

Emerald Tree Boa

Location: South America

Diet: Reptiles, small mammals, birds, and amphibians

Size: 6 feet long

Did You Know?

The bright green coloring of the emerald tree boa makes it hard to see against the leaves of the rainforest trees. This camouflage comes in handy as the snake hunts its prey!

This long, muscular snake has a large head, bright green scales, white markings, and a yellow underside. It spends its life coiled around branches in the rainforest.

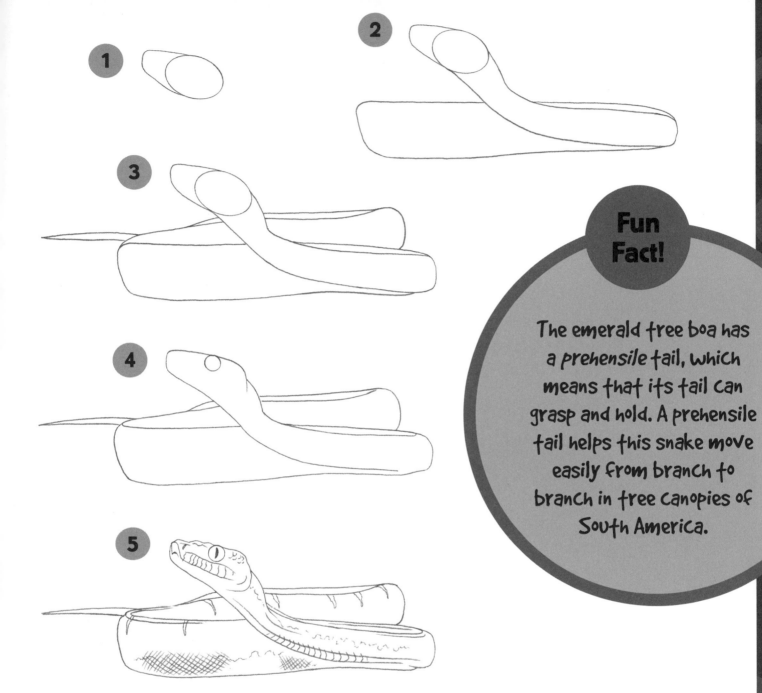

Fun Fact!

The emerald tree boa has a prehensile tail, which means that its tail can grasp and hold. A prehensile tail helps this snake move easily from branch to branch in tree canopies of South America.

Giant Panda

Details

Size: 5 feet long
Weight: 300 pounds
Diet: Bamboo shoots
and leaves
Location: China

Did You Know?

The panda's diet of bamboo shoots and leaves is low in nutrition. Because of this, they must eat about 30 pounds of bamboo per day.

The giant panda is an Asian bear that lives in the mountainous bamboo forests of central China. This solitary creature is known for its distinct black-and-white coat.

Fun Fact!

Pandas are born blind with pink skin and white hair! Their black-and-white coats begin to develop about two weeks after birth.

Chimpanzee

Size: 5 feet tall

Diet: Fruit, berries, nuts, seeds, leaves, and occasionally eggs and small animals

Did You Know?

Chimpanzees teach their young how to make and use tools! For example, they use rocks to crack open nutshells and sticks to probe for insects, such as ants and termites.

Weight: 120 pounds

Location: Africa

With large, rounded ears, a hairless face, and a humanlike body, the chimpanzee is an intelligent primate that lives in the rainforests of equatorial Africa.

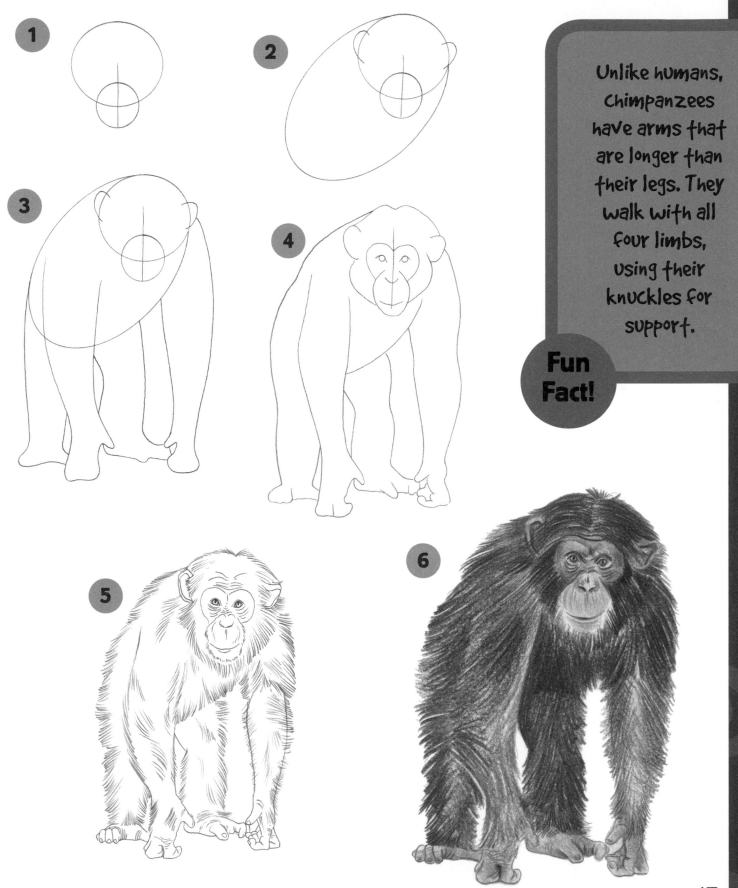

Fun Fact!

Unlike humans, chimpanzees have arms that are longer than their legs. They walk with all four limbs, using their knuckles for support.

Giraffe

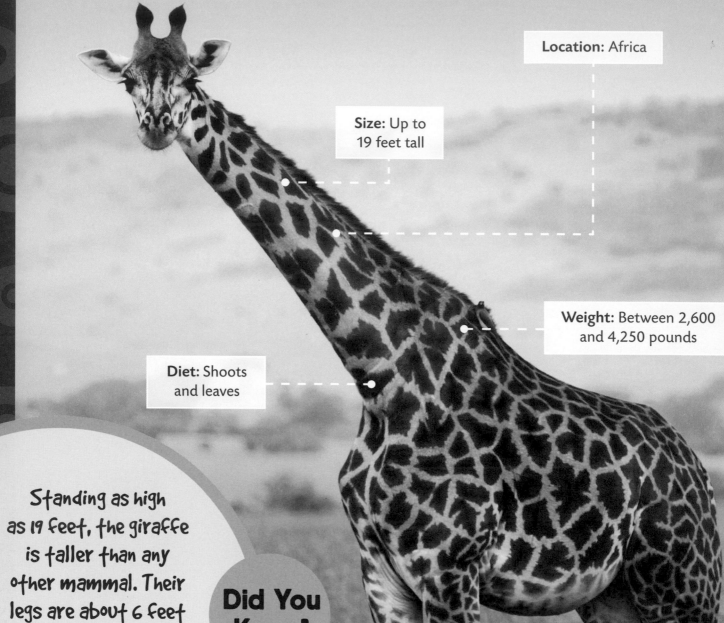

Location: Africa

Size: Up to 19 feet tall

Weight: Between 2,600 and 4,250 pounds

Diet: Shoots and leaves

Did You Know?

Standing as high as 19 feet, the giraffe is taller than any other mammal. Their legs are about 6 feet tall, and their necks are about 5 feet long. Giraffes even have tongues that can reach 20 inches in length!

The giraffe is a hoofed animal known for its tall legs, long neck, and spotted coat. It roams the African savannas as it feeds on the leaves and buds of tall trees.

Mini Quiz

What color is a giraffe's tongue?
A. Green
B. Blue-gray
C. White
D. Pink

(Answer on page 64)

1

2

3

4

5

6

19

Bat

Wingspan: 2.5 inches to 5 feet

Location: Worldwide, except Antarctica

Weight: Less than an ounce up to 2.5 pounds

Diet: Insects and fruit

Did You Know?

Ever heard the saying "blind as a bat?" Bats are born blind, but they do not stay that way forever! Adult bats actually have good vision, which they combine with echolocation (the ability to locate objects using sound) to hunt effectively at twilight and dawn.

A bat generally has a furry body, thin wings, and large, pointed ears. This well-adapted critter can be found on nearly every continent!

Mini Quiz

True or False:
Bats are the only
flying mammals
on earth.

(Answer on page 64)

21

Polar Bear

Details

Size: 8 feet long
Weight: Up to 1,600 pounds
Diet: Seals and some small whales
Location: The Arctic

Did You Know?

Polar bears use broken sheets of ice to travel across the ocean. As global warming continues, their habitat is in danger. Studies say that by 2050, the world's population of polar bears could be one third of what it is today.

The polar bear is a large, powerful Arctic beast. Its thick, white coat and webbed feet make it well adapted to life in snow and icy waters.

Fun Fact! Polar bear feet are not only webbed for swimming, but also have sharp claws and hairs on the bottom to help the bears walk on snow and ice. The claws are also important for capturing prey.

Goat

Size: Up to 2 feet tall at the shoulder

Weight: 60 to 350 pounds

Diet: Hay and grains

Location: Worldwide, except Antarctica

Did You Know?

The largest goat in the world is the Boer goat from South Africa. With red and white coats, lop ears, and strong bodies, males of this species can reach up to 350 pounds!

The goat is a mild-mannered, hoofed animal with wide-set eyes and backward-arching horns. Some goats have long, floppy ears, and some even have beards!

1

2

3

4

5

6

Greater Flamingo

Location: Africa, Asia, and Southern Europe

Size: 4.5 feet tall

Weight: 8 pounds

Diet: Algae, small fish, and invertebrates

Did You Know?

flamingos are often seen standing on just one of their sticklike legs. Scientists have discovered that this habit helps the flamingo conserve body heat, keeping it warm while only one foot stands in the cold water.

The greater flamingo is a distinct bird with pink feathers, long legs, S-shaped neck, and a curved, black-tipped beak.

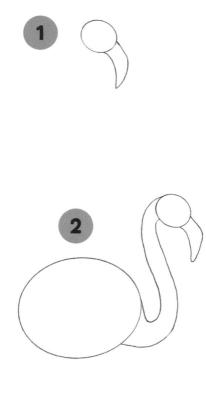

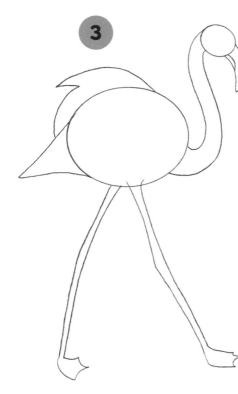

Fun Fact!

When you look at a flamingo wading in the marshes, it appears that their "knees" bend the wrong way. However, these are ankles! flamingos do have knees, but they are covered by its feathers.

Koala

Size: 3 feet long

Location: Australia

Weight: 30 pounds

Diet: Leaves

Did You Know?

Some people may call koalas "bears," but they are actually marsupials! A female marsupial carries its babies in a belly pouch until they are large and strong enough for the world. A baby koala usually stays in its mother's pouch for the first six months of life.

This soft, furry animal has a tall, flat nose; large, round ears; and big, sharp claws. It lives a quiet life in the trees of eastern Australia.

Mini Quiz

What color eyes does the koala have?
A. Blue
B. Red
C. Brown
D. Yellow

(Answer on page 64)

White-Faced Owl

Location: Africa

Size: 10 inches long

Diet: Insects, birds, reptiles, and rodents

Weight: 0.5 pound

Fun Fact!

There are two species of this owl: the northern white-faced owl and the southern white-faced owl. They have subtle differences in coloring, size, and location within Africa. They were once considered one species called the "white-faced scops owl."

The white-faced owl has tufted ears, piercing red-orange eyes, and a plumage of gray, white, and black feathers. It lives in the savannas and woodlands of Africa.

Mini Quiz

How many eyelids does an owl have?
A. 0
B. 1
C. 2
D. 3

(Answer on page 64)

Green Tree Frog

Diet: Insects

Did You Know?

Mood, temperature, and lighting can affect the color of the tree frog's skin. It can range from a light yellow-green to dark olive tones.

Size: 2.25 inches long

Location: Worldwide, except Antarctica

This amphibian is bright green with a yellow stripe along each side of its body. It is known for its long digits and limbs that are great for swimming and climbing.

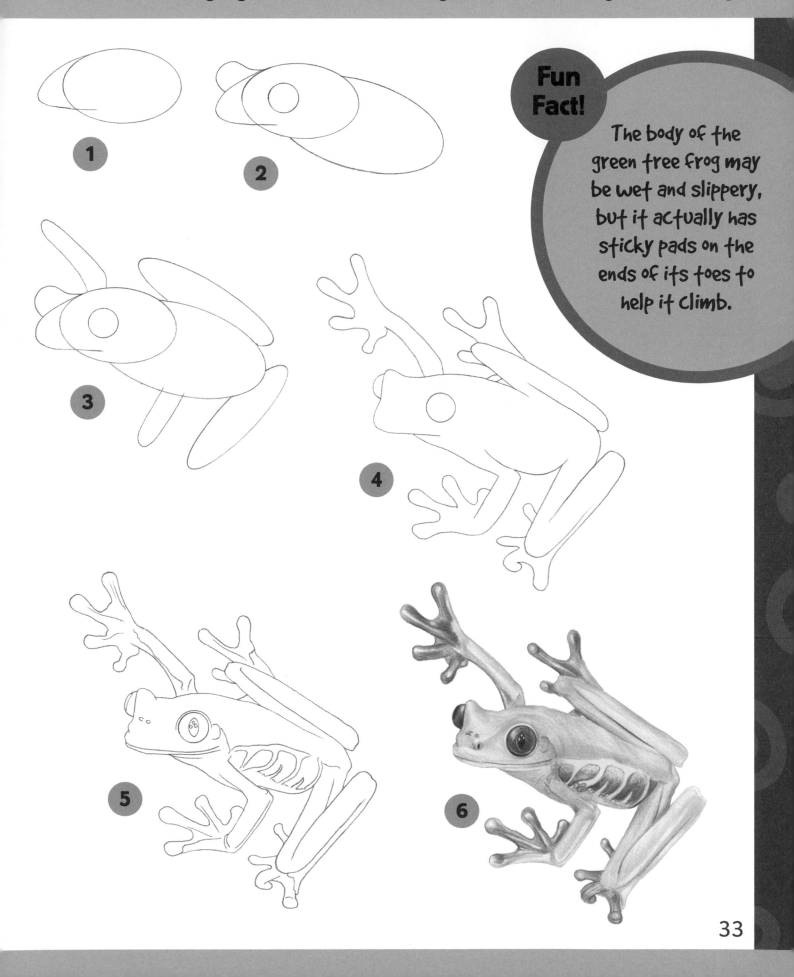

Fun Fact!

The body of the green tree frog may be wet and slippery, but it actually has sticky pads on the ends of its toes to help it climb.

Bactrian Camel

Details

Size: 7 feet tall
Weight: 1,800 pounds
Diet: Vegetation
Location: Asia

Did You Know?

The Bactrian camel's two humps are full of fat, which gives it energy and water during long periods without food or drink. The camel can retain an impressive amount of water—in one sitting, a thirsty camel can soak up to 30 gallons!

This two-humped, wild camel roams the harsh Gobi Desert.
It has bushy eyebrows, large footpads, and a shaggy coat of hair.

Mini Quiz

True or false:
A Bactrian camel can survive without water for up to six months.

(Answer on page 64)

35

Western Lowland Gorilla

Size: 5 feet tall

Did You Know?

The gorilla is the largest primate in the world. The western lowland gorilla, however, is the smallest subspecies of gorilla. Other subspecies include the mountain gorilla, eastern lowland, and cross river gorilla.

Diet: Shoots, leaves, and other vegetation

Weight: 400 pounds

This intelligent animal has a prominent brow, long arms, and black hair and skin. It lives in the rainforests of Africa between the Cameroon and the Congo River.

Fun Fact! A gorilla's face, hands, and feet do not have hair! Also, a mature male does not have hair on its chest.

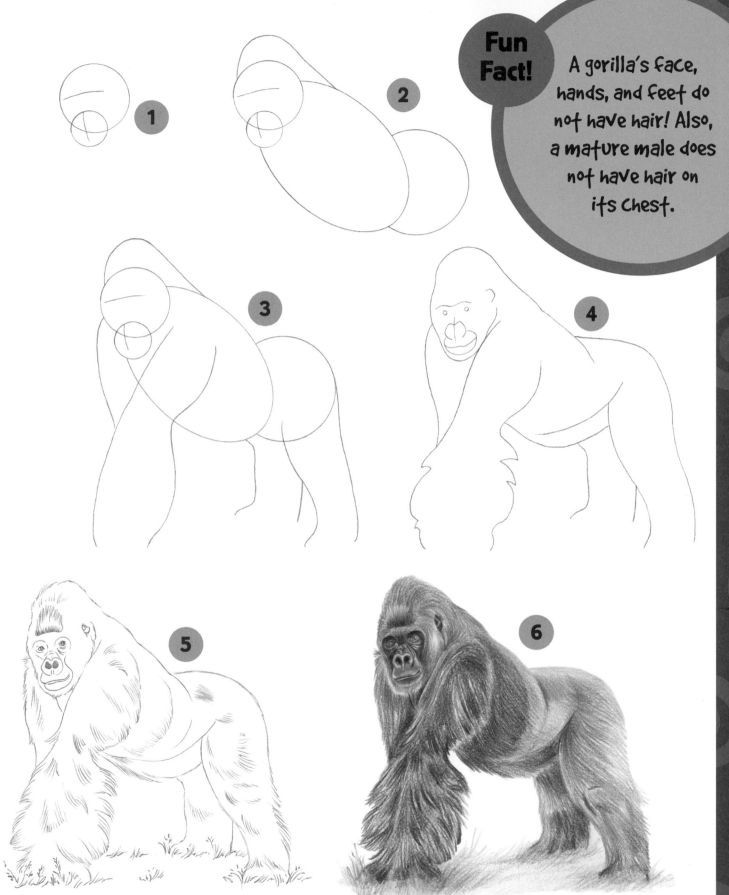

Alligator

Did You Know?

The skin of an alligator's back contains hard, bony plates. These osteoderms help protect the alligator's organs from harm by predators, which include large cats and some birds.

Location: Southeastern United States

Weight: 800 pounds

Size: 20 feet long

Diet: Small animals such as fish, frogs, turtles, birds, and more

The alligator is a large reptile with four short limbs, a long snout, sharp teeth, tough skin, and a flat, powerful tail.

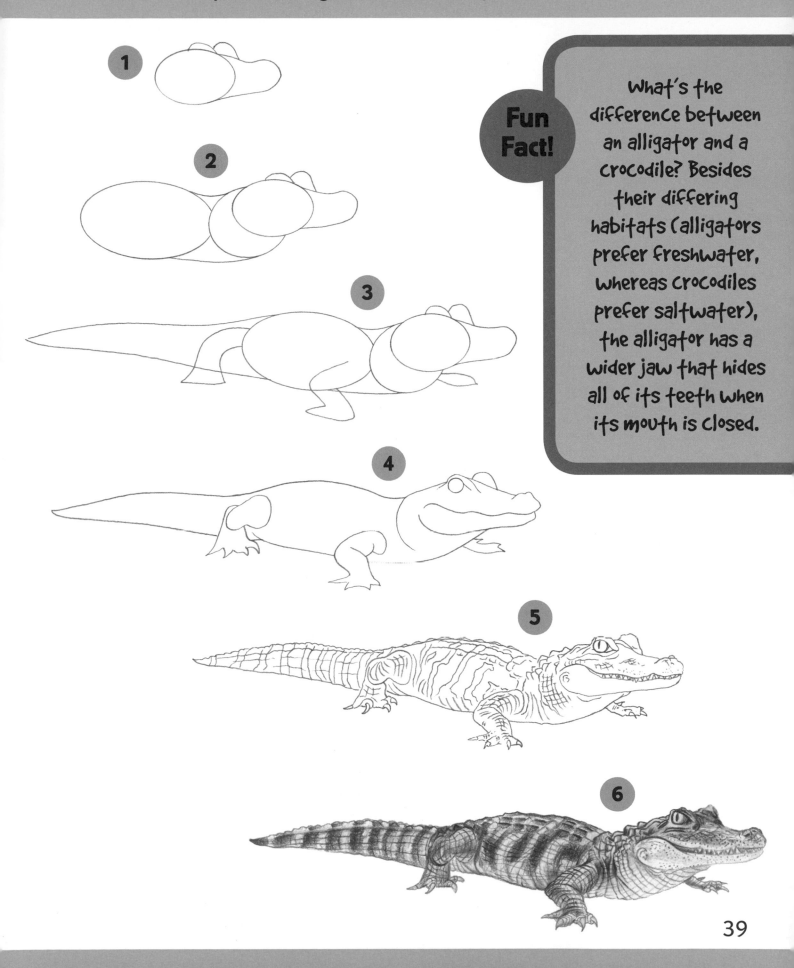

Fun Fact!

What's the difference between an alligator and a crocodile? Besides their differing habitats (alligators prefer freshwater, whereas crocodiles prefer saltwater), the alligator has a wider jaw that hides all of its teeth when its mouth is closed.

39

Wallaby

Size: 3 feet long

Location: Australia and nearby islands

Weight: Up to 50 pounds

Diet: Grasses and plants

Did You Know?

Wallabies live in a variety of habitats, from deserts and rocky areas to forests and scrubs. The smallest species of wallaby is a forest dweller of New Guinea and weighs only 3.5 pounds!

Similar to a kangaroo in appearance, the wallaby has brown and gray fur, small forearms, powerful hind legs, and a long, thick tail.

1

2

3

4

5

6

Mini Quiz

Wallabies are marsupials, which means the females...
A. Lay eggs
B. Give birth to independent babies
C. Carry their babies in a pouch
D. Are cold-blooded

(Answer on page 64)

41

Tiger

Details

Size: 10 feet long
Weight: 600 pounds
Diet: Wild pigs, deer, water
buffalo, and
other animals
Location: Asia

Mini Quiz

Which of the following is the
largest species of tiger?
A. Bengal tiger
B. Malayan tiger
C. Siberian tiger
D. Javan tiger

(Answer on page 64)

The tiger is the largest wildcat on Earth. It has big paws, a cheek ruff, and a reddish coat with striking black-and-white markings.

Fun Fact!

You may have heard that cats dislike water, but that's not the case with tigers! These beasts are great swimmers that often beat the heat by swimming in streams and ponds.

Giant Tortoise

Size: 4 feet long

Weight: 475 pounds

Diet: Cactus, grasses, and leaves

Giant tortoises generally live longer than humans. The oldest tortoise known to man lived to be 152 years old!

Fun Fact!

Location: Galápagos Islands

Known as the largest tortoise on the planet, the giant tortoise of the Galápagos has a long neck, thick limbs, scaly skin, and a hard, saddle-shaped shell.

Mini Quiz

How long can a giant tortoise go without food or water?
A. 2 weeks
B. 6 months
C. 1 year
D. 5 years

(Answer on page 64)

45

Emu

Size: 5 feet tall

Diet: Fruits, vegetables, grasses, grains, insects, and worms

Weight: 100 pounds

Location: Australia

Did You Know?

The emu is a "flightless" bird, which means that—despite having wings—it cannot fly. Other flightless birds include the penguin and the ostrich.

The emu is a large Australian bird with a long neck, a triangular beak, and a plumage of brown feathers. Their long, strong legs make them swift runners.

Fun Fact!

The emu has two sets of eyelids! It uses one set for blinking and the other for keeping its eyes free of sand and other particles.

Black Rhino

Sadly, the black rhino is an endangered species. Many have been hunted for their horns, as some cultures use them in medicines. There are currently about 5,000 black rhinos left in the wild.

Did You Know?

Location: Africa

Size: 5 feet tall at the shoulder

Diet: Leaves and fruit

Weight: Up to 2,900 pounds

This large, gray-skinned mammal has a thick body, a humped neck, and a pointed upper lip. It also has two curved horns on its nasal bridge.

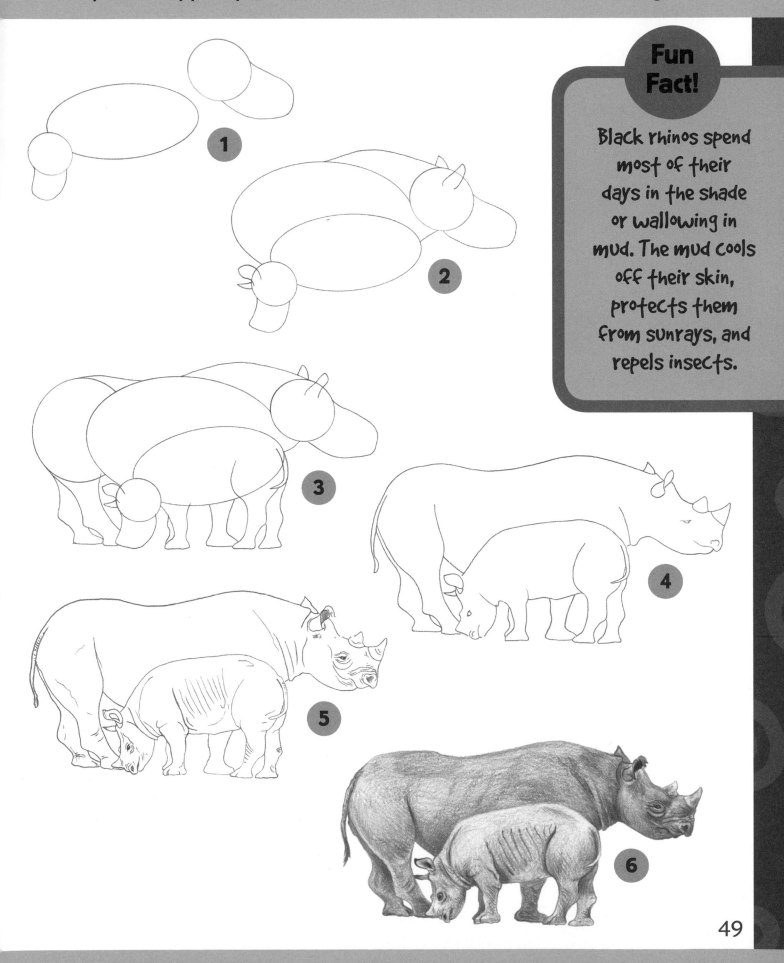

Fun Fact!

Black rhinos spend most of their days in the shade or wallowing in mud. The mud cools off their skin, protects them from sunrays, and repels insects.

Golden Eagle

Details

Size: 3 feet long
Weight: 10 pounds
Diet: Rodents, birds, fish, and other small animals
Location: North America, Europe, Asia, and North Africa

Mini Quiz

What is the average wingspan of the golden eagle?
A. 2.5 feet
B. 5 feet
C. 7.5 feet
D. 10 feet

(Answer on page 64)

The majestic golden eagle is a fast-flying bird with a hooked beak, powerful talons, brown feathers, and golden coloring on its head and neck.

Fun Fact!
The golden eagle is the national bird of Mexico.

Ring-Tailed Lemur

Location: Madagascar

Size: 17 inches long

Diet: Fruit, leaves, flowers, and tree bark

Did You Know?

Although the ring-tailed lemur looks like a relative of the raccoon, it's actually a primate and is more closely related to a monkey.

Weight: 7 pounds

The ring-tailed lemur has a small, pointy face and golden-colored eyes. It is named after the white and black bands around its long, bushy tail.

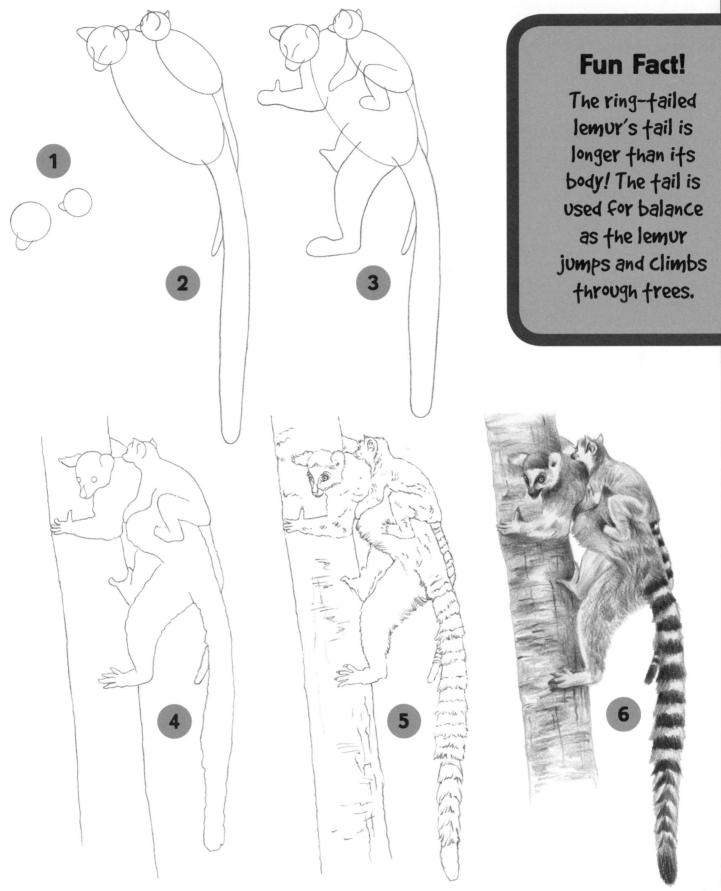

1

2

3

4

5

6

Fun Fact!

The ring-tailed lemur's tail is longer than its body! The tail is used for balance as the lemur jumps and climbs through trees.

Komodo Dragon

Details

Size: 10 feet long
Weight: 300 pounds
Diet: Deer, pigs, water buffalo, eggs, and other animals
Location: Indonesian Islands

Did You Know?

The komodo dragon's excellent sense of smell comes from its tongue! Similar to a snake, this lizard sticks out its lengthy, forked tongue to sample the air, which helps it find prey from far distances.

This large, fierce reptile has scaly skin, a thick tail, sharp claws and teeth, muscular limbs, and a long, yellow tongue.

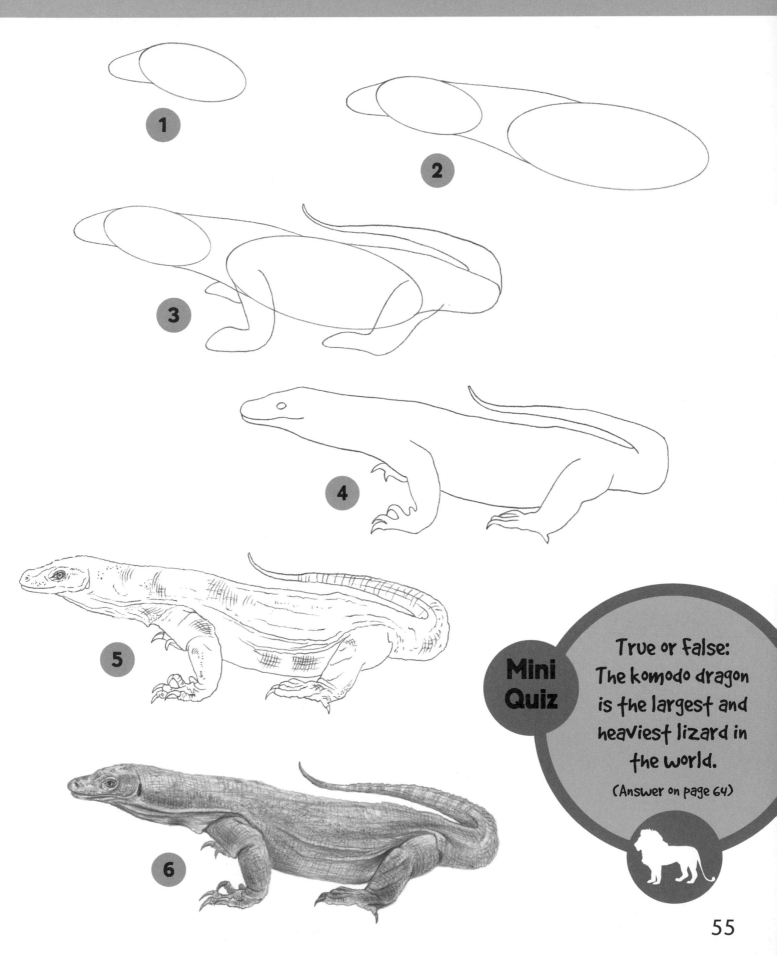

Mini Quiz

True or false: The komodo dragon is the largest and heaviest lizard in the world.

(Answer on page 64)

Pygmy Hippo

Details

Size: 2.5 feet tall
Weight: 500 pounds
Diet: Leaves, ferns, roots, grasses, and fruits
Location: Western Africa

Fun Fact!

When a pygmy hippo goes underwater, its ears and nose close to prevent water from entering!

The pygmy hippo has dark skin, a rounded body, small ears, and bulging eyes.
To keep their skin wet, they live near swamps, rivers, and streams.

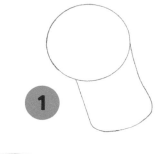

1

2

3

4

5

6

Did You Know?

The thick skin of the pygmy hippo secretes a red foamy substance, which can give their greenish gray skin a pink tint. Scientists are unsure of the secretion's purpose, but some believe it protects the skin from the harsh rays of the sun, acting like a natural sunscreen.

Porcupine

Size:
3 feet long

Location: North America, South America, Europe, Asia, and Africa

Weight:
30 pounds

A porcupine's sharp, hollow quills are made of keratin—the same substance that makes up our hair and fingernails. These quills usually rest flat against the back, but they stand up when the porcupine is threatened.

Did You Know?

Diet: Herbs, leaves, bark, and twigs

This prickly rodent has a triangular face, short limbs, and a back covered in quills. It is found everywhere in the world except Antarctica and Australia.

Grizzly Bear

Details

Size: Up to 8 feet tall
Weight: Up to 800 pounds
Diet: Fish, small animals, nuts, berries, fruit, and leaves.
Location: North America

Did You Know?

Like all bears, grizzlies bulk up on fattening food during the summer months. During the winter months, they dig out warm dens and settle into a deep sleep called "hibernation." To conserve energy, their heart rates decrease and their body temperatures drop—they even stop going to the bathroom!

This large bear has round ears, small eyes, and a coat of brown, grizzled fur. Its giant claws, sharp teeth, and strong jaws make it a fierce predator.

Fun Fact!

Grizzly bears have good eyesight, like humans, but they have a much more developed sense of smell—even better than a bloodhound's!

Gr vy's Zebr

Size: Up to 5 feet tall at the shoulder

Location: Africa

Weight: 900 pounds

Fun Fact!

You'd never know it by their appearance, but zebras actually have black skin under their coat of fur!

Diet: Grasses and other vegetation

This horselike African animal has a long muzzle, rounded ears, distinct black-and-white striped coat, and mane that stands up on the back of its neck.

Mini Quiz

What is another name for the Grevy's zebra?
A. Imperial zebra
B. Mountain zebra
C. Plains zebra
D. Grasslands zebra

(Answer on page 64)

63

Mini Quiz Answers

Page 9: A. A group of lions is called a "pride."

Page 19: B. A giraffe's tongue is blue-gray.

Page 21: True. Bats are the only mammals that can fly.

Page 29: C. Most koalas have brown eyes, but a very small percentage has blue eyes.

Page 31: D. Owls have three eyelids.

Page 35: True. Thanks to its ability to store fat, the Bactrian camel can survive for six months without water.

Page 41: C. A marsupial carries his young in a pouch.

Page 42: C. The Siberian tiger is the largest of all tiger species and can weigh up to 660 pounds.

Page 45: C. A giant tortoise can go about 1 year without food or water.

Page 50: C. The average wingspan of the golden eagle is a whopping 7.5 feet.

Page 55: True. The komodo dragon is the largest and heaviest lizard in the world.

Page 63: A. Another name for Grevy's zebra is the Imperial zebra.